49 Trout Streams of Southern Colorado

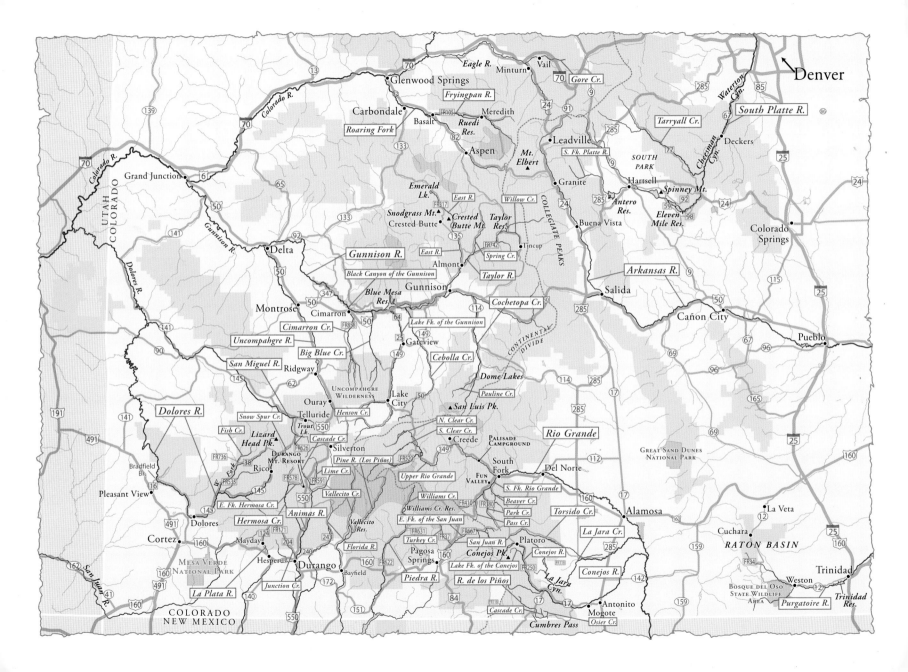

49 TROUT STREAMS
of SOUTHERN COLORADO

Mark D. Williams
W. Chad McPhail

UNIVERSITY OF NEW MEXICO PRESS
Albuquerque

Printed in Singapore.
18 17 16 15 14 13   1 2 3 4 5 6

Library of Congress Cataloging-in-Publication Data

Williams, Mark D., 1960–
49 trout streams of southern Colorado / Mark D. Williams and W. Chad McPhail.
p. cm.
ISBN 978-0-8263-5137-1 (pbk. : alk. paper) — ISBN 978-0-8263-5138-8 (electronic)
1. Trout fishing—Colorado—Guidebooks. 2. Fly fishing—Colorado—Guidebooks.
3. Rivers—Colorado—Guidebooks. I. McPhail, W. Chad. II. Title. III.
Title: Forty-nine trout streams of southern Colorado.
SH687.W565 2013
799.17'5709788—dc23
2012026257

BOOK DESIGN AND TYPE COMPOSITION by Catherine Leonardo
Composed in Adobe Garamond Pro 10.3/13.4
Display type is Ex Ponto Pro

Contents

We've been lucky. We've been lucky that we have been able to fish and get paid to write about it. We've been lucky to have great families and great friends (who also get to fish with us). We've been lucky enough to fish thousands of miles of rivers around the country and around the world. And of all the waters in all the world, we find ourselves returning to those in southern Colorado more than any others.

Southern Colorado has all the intangibles. There's just something special about this amazingly gorgeous region of the Southwest. The epic flats of the San Luis Valley, the craggy peaks near Ridgway, the high-desert badlands near Durango, the ethereal wilderness of Saguache . . . and seeping from all of these areas an endless number of streams and rivers in which to fish. Think it was easy selecting only forty-nine rivers from the hundreds of our favorites in southern Colorado? Think again. We did our best, but we also tried to mix things up. We started this project following the pattern in UNM Press's very successful title *49 Trout Streams of New Mexico*. Unfortunately for literary exactitude but fortunately for fisherman, there are far more than forty-nine streams in southern Colorado to tempt anglers, so we have added seven bonus streams where fishermen can find remote Colorado waters that offer lively days of fishing for wild native trout.

Most fly fishing books contain only black-and-white photos and lots of text, our earlier books included. Inspired by *49 Trout Streams of New Mexico*, we wanted to create a fly fishing book with minimal text and exceptional color shots.

(Editor in Chief Clark Whitehorn at UNM Press shared our enthusiasm and agreed to the project. Thanks, Clark.) Multiple color photos can show anglers more about whether or not they want to fish a river, as well as how to fish it, than any smartly written paragraph they will ever read. So, we chose our five or so favorite photos to represent each of these rivers. Whittling these pictures down to five from hundreds and even thousands was difficult—sometimes painful—and other times seemingly impossible. We truly hope you enjoy the photographs we've decided on.

Selected flies have been assigned to each river as well, but we didn't always go with the obvious default pattern, the usual suspect, or the fly the local fly shop suggests to every average Joe inquiring what to cast. We picked patterns that have worked for us in the past, flies that surprised us, patterns that caught the big ones, and flies that landed dozens of trout in a single hour. Obvious flies are just that—obvious. Instead, we opted to insert a few that might surprise you on the water.

Furthermore, we have also included some rather delicate, lesser-known, high-country streams that, if over-trafficked, might suffer being overfished. We debated at great length over many of these, striking some from the very get-go and leaving only a select handful for whatever reason. If you're wondering why some of your favorite smaller waters aren't presented here, this process of elimination may explain why.

Please have fun thumbing through the book. Hopefully, with the help of a good map, and a decent weather report, planning your next southern Colorado fly fishing endeavor will prove much more informative, visual, and exciting.

Greenback beadhead nymph

When the Spanish explorers came here, they named this boisterous river "Rio de las Animas Perdidas," which translates to "River of the Lost Souls." Not all that long ago, the Animas River was thought to be just another lost soul, another great river in decline. And it was. Formerly one of the top brown trout fisheries in the West, most of the Animas River has now recovered from years of abuse from mining pollution. This wild freestone river flows through awe-inspiring southwestern scenery, through wide valleys and steep canyons, past rugged mountains and aspen and pine forests, continuing south past cottonwoods and on into New Mexico—it's one of the last free-flowing rivers in the West. Let's be realistic: how often can you find a blue-ribbon fishery in the middle of a town, especially a town as cool as Durango?

The trout that reside in the Animas are known for their athleticism and heft. You can fish (and catch fish) all through town, too, as there is quality water and lots of public access.

Designated a Gold Medal Water, the Animas fishes amazingly well from February to April and again after runoff—which can be threateningly high and roily—but our favorite time is in fall, when the browns are active and the leaves are changing. From Lightner Creek to Purple Cliffs, use artificial flies and lures only. The bag and possession limit for trout is two fish, sixteen inches or longer. Watch signage so you don't trespass, as there is a patchwork of private and public access areas.

Experience wilderness angling unlike anywhere else in the Southwest by riding the steam-powered Durango-Silverton Narrow Gauge Railroad and getting dropped off in the middle of some of the wildest country anywhere. You can do this on your own, but we recommend hiring a guide. You can fish until the afternoon Silverton train comes back or spend the night (or two) and the train will take you back to civilization.

Chartreuse humpy

Described by avid river rafters as a "mild to wild" river, the Arkansas offers anglers of every skill level an opportunity and a challenge. Originating near the legendary mining town of Leadville, the upper Arkansas begins as a collection of tributaries below Mount Elbert, the highest Rocky Mountain peak in North America at 14,433 feet above sea level, and moves across four states until converging with the mighty Mississippi.

By the time the Arkansas reaches Granite, it quickly gains volume, finding a scenic path along the eastern slopes of the Collegiate Peaks, where river rafting and kayaking are popular activities. Many anglers also prefer this same stretch of river from Granite to Buena Vista and Salida, with cottonwoods and meadows, plentiful pullouts and parking areas, and easily waded stretches.

Brown trout were introduced into the Arkansas River in the 1800s and now represent about 80 percent of the river's trout community, with most averaging twelve inches and the occasional brown growing to more than twenty inches. A species of rainbow trout resistant to whirling disease has also been stocked since 2009 in order to establish species diversity and self-sustaining populations.

Important insect hatches include blue-winged olives from mid-March to mid-May; the Mother's Day caddis from mid-April to mid-May; stoneflies, various mayflies, and grasshoppers from summer through fall; and midges all winter long. It's a great fall getaway. The trees range from cottonwood to spruce to lodgepole pine to aspen in the highest elevations.

As most of the Arkansas is safe to wade or fish from the bank, floating this river is perhaps the best way to experience its diversity and character. There are many guides and outfitters in the region geared up for the trout-fishing trip of a lifetime. Follow U.S. 24 south from Leadville to U.S. 285. U.S. 285 parallels the river in a southerly direction to CO 291, which then follows the Arkansas to Salida. U.S. 50 follows the river easterly from Salida to Cañon City.

Peacock humpy Wulff

We had fished all around Beaver Creek for decades, and it wasn't till our *Eat, Fish, Sleep* book that we took time to angle this beautiful stream just south of Southfork. One of our favorite places to fish in southern Colorado is now the upper meadows of this Rio Grande feeder creek.

The river is green and clear near the lower section, close to the campgrounds. The water is out of a postcard, but you won't catch many trout here. Too many anglers. Move upstream toward the reservoir (and above) to increase your catch rate. In the lower reaches, you fish under ponderosa pines, spruces, and firs, but in the headwaters, aspens come up to the meadows. You can fish the less-shaded canyon waters, but you'll have to get into the water and wade up because it's tough to scramble down. Don't miss out on driving several miles upstream till the stream flows back and forth through verdant meadows. Beginning angler's paradise.

If you love small streams, try Cross Creek and Race Creek, both feeder streams to Beaver Creek. Cross Creek is willowy and tight, but if you can drop a fly on the water, you'll catch brooks and browns. McPhail caught a beautiful seventeen-inch brown out of a small pool, slipping and falling on his backside while landing it. From South Fork, at the intersection of CO 149 and U.S. 160, take U.S. 160 west 1.4 miles to the Beaver Creek Road sign. Turn left at the sign onto Beaver Creek Road and go 3.1 miles to campground sign. Turn right at sign and go 0.1 miles to another campground sign.

Lime Wulff

A classic high-country meadow stream, Big Blue Creek runs northerly toward a marriage with the Gunnison River drainage. The clear blue stream winds back and forth for mile after mile through a wide glacial valley, occasionally slowing to form a beaver pond or deep cut bank pool. The creek doesn't hold any whoppers, so your reason for fishing at ten thousand feet will have to be pristine scenery, wild trout, and clean air.

Big Blue Creek and two feeder streams, Soldier Creek and Fall Creek, run through the eastern section of the Uncompahgre Wilderness, past groves of colorful, singing aspens and forests of spruce and fir. These creeks are three of the prettiest small trout streams in Colorado, perfect for fishing dry flies. If you drive the twelve miles of dirt road back to Big Blue Campground, you'll see the best scenery in the Gunnison area. Be sure to check out the beaver ponds near the campground for some challenging light-leader fishing. The Big Blue has good beaver ponds, nice pools, and undercut banks, and it offers anglers a chance to catch brooks and cutthroats seven to fourteen inches long (you'll catch mostly brookies in the middle and lower sections). Miss this stream and you'll miss the true flavor of this sparsely populated area of Colorado. Don't pass Soldier Creek without stopping to dap a few flies in it. Great for beginning fly fishers.

Getting to this paradise involves a long drive on a one-lane road. We recommend a four-wheel-drive auto but a high-clearance two-wheel-drive vehicle is OK under dry conditions. We have taken low-slung passenger cars up this sinuous road but we never felt entirely comfortable. Travel north from Lake City on CO 149 eleven miles and look for the Big Blue Campground sign. Turn left and take your time to soak in the aspen stands, grassy meadows, and wildlife. Switchback after switchback makes for a slow eleven-mile drive before you cross Soldier Creek and reach Big Blue Trailhead and Campground.

In the fields and along the trails, look for colorful flora such as lupine, paintbrush, valerian, and many others. Another option for adventurous driver-anglers is to come in from Nellie Creek.

Red-ribbed black beadhead stonefly

What do you get? Remoteness, solitude, a spectacular gorge, and abundant wildlife, including eagles. In the Black Canyon of the Gunnison, once an angler completes the difficult eight-hour descent into the canyon, the next takeout point is two to three days away as one floats the river. The Black Canyon of the Gunnison River has more numbers of big trout (sixteen to twenty-five inches) than any other water in the state. Rainbows and browns over four or five pounds are not uncommon.

Granite walls rise up from the banks, caressing the tiny sliver of blue sky above. Sometimes, you'll see aspen daisies dotting the banks. Cold, blue-green, clear, big water. The river and the canyon are spectacular. Breathlessly beautiful. The Black Canyon of the Gunnison River.

There are trails to the Black Canyon but they are either strenuous or dangerous—steep, winding, and narrow, with two-thousand-foot drop-offs—you get the picture. We recommend hiring a guide for a float trip. On your first go, forty-eight miles of canyon is just too much to overcome. Plus, guides will know this river and fishing conditions much better than you. Because the river is so tough to reach, it is a highly productive fishery. The Gunnison River rainbows are among the feistiest and most colorful we've ever caught. But where we used to catch more rainbows than browns, it's about even now and the browns are getting bigger on average.

The Black Canyon, except in times of big stone hatches, is not a dry fly river. You nymph with a variety of subsurface offerings, including weighted stonefly nymphs, or you crash big streamers. Hire a guide—don't risk the trails to the river. Spend two to three days in the canyon in a once-in-a-lifetime trip. You can find guides in Montrose, Gunnison, and Telluride.

High at the top of the canyon, you find juniper and piñon pine, but down the slopes and along the river, you find pockets of Douglas fir and aspen trees. Chokecherry, box elder, and narrow-leaf cottonwood crowd the riverbank.

To get to the South Rim of the canyon, travel east on U.S. 50 from Montrose or west on U.S. 50 from Cimarron until you come to CO 347. Turn north on CO 347 and drive six miles to the park entrance. An entrance fee of fifteen dollars per vehicle is charged at the South Rim entrance station and the North Rim ranger station of Black Canyon. It covers all persons in a single, private, noncommercial vehicle and is valid for seven calendar days.

Black Canyon of the Gunnison River

PMX (a rubber-legged
Stimulator with hi-vis)

risky little stream that feeds into the Animas north of Durango. Cascade Creek is one of the slipperiest creeks we've ever fished, so if you have cleated waders, wear 'em. A wading stick is a super idea. The bouncy creek holds brook and rainbow trout, and its pocket water and riffles are ideal for teaching a beginning fly fisher or spending an afternoon tossing dry flies. Pack a fly box with attractor flies, wear your shorts and wading boots, and go out for a thirty-fish day. Nothing big, all wild.

The upper reaches are accessed a couple of miles north of Durango Mountain Resort, running alongside FR 785. A few miles up, you'll need a four-wheel-drive vehicle. The lower four miles are accessed by the Purgatory Trail (FT 511) before the creek enters the Animas River. The canyon is not for the faint of heart, but if you try it, you'll have big pools and wild trout all to your lonesome.

Cascade Creek (Animas)

Hot butt Stimulator

Splashing beneath the picturesque train bridge a few miles west of Osier Station, 2.5 miles of Cascade Creek (6 miles east of Cumbres Pass from the headwaters to the confluence with Rio de los Pinos) are designated by the state of Colorado as Wild Trout Water.

Cascade Creek is isolated and steeped in history. There are several routes, none of which are boring or without scenery. Perhaps the most favored route to Cascade Creek is via train on the Cumbres & Toltec Scenic Railroad. Plans can be made through the railway to be dropped off and picked up at a designated point. This allows backpacking fly fishers an outdoor excursion unlike any other in the state. The train arrives at Osier about midday each day during the summer.

Small, shallow, and loaded with drop pools, Cascade Creek will surprise anglers with unsuspecting deep plunges hiding Rio Grande cutthroats the perfect size for 1-weights to 3-weights. Though brushy in spots and shallow in others, the challenge of duping wild, native trout with attractor dry flies in the backcountry is the allure of streams such as Cascade Creek. Fishing allowed only with flies or lures.

Travel west from Antonito on CO 17. After about 10 miles, turn south on FR 103, also signed as Road D-5. Follow the road across a mesa to Osier Station. You'll see a sign pointing to Osier Creek at the train station. To get to Cascade Creek, follow the train tracks to the west of Osier, about 1.5 miles. To get to the headwaters of both creeks, turn off of FR 103 (before Osier) onto FR 107 and travel north.

Cascade Creek (Rio de los Pinos)

Madame X

*P*ronounced *say-vo-ya*, Cebolla Creek is one of the unsung trout streams in the state—small, off the beaten path, a spring-fed jewel full of wild brown and brook trout. Anglers can catch any of four species from its headwaters at Spring Creek Pass downstream to where it enters Blue Mesa Reservoir.

The creek is no stranger to angling pressure during the summer. Despite the numbers of fishers, Cebolla Creek stands up well. While the stream is less than ten feet wide near the headwaters, it collects numerous feeder creeks along its way north to Blue Mesa Reservoir and eventually becomes a fair-sized creek.

Cebolla Creek being primarily a brook trout stream in the upper reaches, anglers enjoy dapping and slashing attractor dry flies on its pocket water and plentiful beaver ponds. There are some sections of private water, but anglers can fish in almost ten miles of public water. Trout in this section of the Cebolla are brookies and browns, and they rarely exceed twelve inches. The water south of Cebolla State Wildlife Area is loaded with deep pocket water and nice trout.

As the Cebolla moves midcourse, through a rocky canyon, past aspen- and spruce-forested cliffs, its flow grows and so do the size of its fish. Along its banks, willows can sometimes get in your way. Anglers occasionally tie into a brown over fifteen inches. Another nice thing about the stream is that it fishes well early in the season and into late September. The Cebolla recovers quickly from rainstorms and from runoff, so keep that in mind if the Lake Fork of the Gunnison River swells during either. Insect hatches are frequent on the Cebolla, with heavy populations of both caddis and mayfly. As for fowl, watch for rock wrens, assorted sparrows (Savannah, Lincoln's, and Brewer), and dusky grouse. Elk, deer, and moose work the thick streamside vegetation, so keep your eyes and ears open. We've been startled many times.

Anglers can travel south from Lake City 9.1 miles and get off CO 149 onto Mill Creek Road (CR 50, also known as FR 788). Turn left and go 3 miles on a dirt road until you reach the creek. The road follows the creek.

Cebolla Creek

Adams

The big draw to this river is that so few anglers know about it. We like this Gunnison River feeder creek as a home base for the family or your fishing buddies. Set up camp at one of several sites, and at your disposal, you will have several lakes and no fewer than four legitimate streams full of trout. The trout aren't big, but they are frisky, wild, and catchable.

In the few miles above the stream's confluence with the Gunnison, in the Cimarron State Wildlife Area, you will find the largest, widest parts of the Cimarron skirted by looming cottonwoods mixed with spruce trees. We've seen this section of the river muddy up due to summer rains, but fall is a great time to try for active browns and rainbows. Above Silver Jack Reservoir, in the Uncompahgre Wilderness, you'll find more aspen mixed with spruce and you'll find the West, Middle, and East Forks of Cimarron Creek and to the east of the lake, Little Cimarron Creek. Afternoon rains can also cause the East and Middle Forks to muddy up, but the Little Cimarron clears up quickly. The Middle and West Forks have solid access from forest service roads, but the East Fork requires you to hike up TR 228.

This is bear country—a wide valley surrounded by forest in the middle of nowhere. While you have ample campgrounds, no services are close. From Gunnison, take U.S. 50 west, turn south on FR 858. From Ridgway, the Owl Creek Pass Road is one of the most scenic we've ever driven. As a side note, many scenes from the original *True Grit* were shot near here, including the famous dogfall fight scene at the end. From Cimarron, take U.S. 50 east 2.2 miles to the forest access/Silver Jack Reservoir sign. Turn right onto a gravel road and go 6.1 miles to an intersection (RDP 77). Bear left onto RDP 77 (dirt—rocky and rough in places) and go 9.5 miles to campground sign. You can park here.

Cimarron Creek

Parachute hare's ear

Cochetopa Creek

Overshadowed by more notable place names—Gunnison, Salida, and Creede—perhaps no other Colorado stream is as overlooked as Cochetopa Creek.

Trickling from the base of the 14,014-foot San Luis Peak in Saguache County, the upper Cochetopa is a diminutive mountain stream holding sporadic trout, albeit in a stunning alpine setting where the water oxbows through open meadows and aspen stands. But it's the slow, meandering ranch valley stream below that holds the most and largest browns, some twenty inches or more—huge fish for such a little known water. Once you fish it, it will become one of your favorites. Cochetopa is already one of our top streams.

Hairpin bends and steep cut banks characterize the Cochetopa above and below the Dome Lakes, where casting is unobstructed by trees and vegetation. Practice stealthy approaches and tie on long, light leaders and finer tippets than normal. A mix of gravel bars and freestone lanes, it's easily waded, but some pools are deceptively deep. Watch thy step.

Wild Trout Water signs are posted along the entire course, with fishing along the easement of the Coleman lease being some of the most popular and exciting. Lucrative days can be spent on the two miles downstream of the Dome Lakes, where casting a dropper rig trailing a nymph eighteen inches deep brings the deepest fish out of hiding.

Mayflies, caddis, and terrestrials are favorite surface patterns. Stimulators and Madam X patterns always work well in midsummer, trailed by weighted ribbed hare's ears and caddis pupae. Aim for mid-June through early August, as well as September and October fishing in wetter seasons.

From Gunnison, travel east eight miles to CO 114. Travel south about twenty-one miles and turn left at NN-14 Road. The easement is signed. You can gain more access by continuing south on NN-14 Road for about two miles to the KK-14 Road running west. Follow this and look for access.

19

Hairwing green drake sparkle dun

A tail water that doesn't fish quite as technical as many others, the Conejos River ("rabbits" in Spanish) is one of Colorado's most scenic, and one of the Rio Grande's greatest tributaries. From the dam at Platoro Reservoir to the junction with the mighty Rio Grande, the Conejos exhibits every characteristic a trout stream could possess, with a parade of charismatic estuary streams adding to the mix as well.

Throughout its course, huge rogue browns lurch for green drakes, stoneflies, midges, and an entourage of mayfly patterns, with some of the most exciting action occurring in Pinnacle Canyon, where dry-dropper rigs suit up well. Anglers also find world-class rainbow fishing, and native cutthroats in the high country. Dramatic mountains, spires, cliffs, and peaks are surrounded by forests of ponderosa pine and spruce—this is wild scenery. In the lower sections, by Mogote, you'll find juniper and cottonwood trees and less scenic geography—bigger fish but fewer, too.

The Conejos is a ninety-plus-mile hodgepodge of public and private water with the uppermost forty miles (upstream of Antonito) being the best fishing, and most accessible. Mirroring CO 17, numerous pullouts mark designated public fishing locations as well as the fence step-overs along the washboarded FR 250 from the Elk Creek confluence all the way to Platoro. Make sure to hit Elk Creek, the Lake Fork, and Rito Azul while fishing this drainage.

Conejos River

Red copper john

The high-desert countryside of this twelve-mile tail water is rugged and bleak, resembling nothing like a setting for a trout stream—that's part of the charm. Keep your eyes peeled for wildlife: deer, turkeys, eagles, even bears. This tail water has cutthroat, rainbow, and brown trout.

The river is fishable year-round, but spring runoff makes the river brownish-red and swollen. Upstream sections freeze over in winter, but the feeding lanes on the tailrace close to the dam can be productive. Summertime brings great dry fly fishing, and fall has excellent fishing for large browns.

The Dolores tail water is a challenging river with solid hatches and tremendous holding water, but too many anglers make the mistake of not taking the fish seriously. The clear water and educated trout mean that you should use long leaders, be cautious, and match the hatch. In the 1980s, the river was on its way to becoming one of the top tail water fisheries in the West, but drought and mismanagement damaged the fishery. It's good but not great now. And in the winter, you walk in and have the entire river to yourself. The tail water runs through high desert dotted with piñon, scrub oak, and juniper.

But don't miss out on the upper Dolores. Classic freestone mountain waters and aspen and spruce forests make it a must-fish for any small-stream enthusiast. Upstream, camp streamside among subalpine and conifer trees mixed with grassy meadows. Look at the riffles of the main upper Dolores and the West Fork as well as Fish, Stoner, Bear, and Snowspur Creeks.

Travel west from Durango on U.S. 160 about sixty miles, to Cortez. Take U.S. 491 north past the hamlet of Pleasant View, follow the signs, turn right to CR 16, then turn north (left). Veer right toward the river and cross Bradfield Bridge over the Dolores. Lone Dome Road runs along the north side of the river eleven miles to the dam. To reach the upper Dolores, head west from Durango to Cortez on U.S. 160 and go north on CO 145.

Dolores River

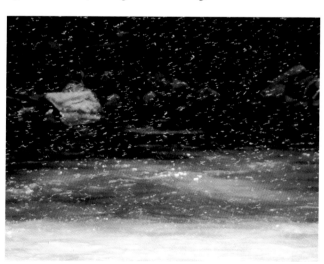

Damselfly nymph beadhead

North of Crested Butte sits a tiny, high-country still water fishery named Emerald Lake. Snowmelt trickles from its southern end, passing the ghost town of Gothic, where the East River picks up steam from tributary creeks with names such as Copper, Cement, and Roaring Judy.

Completely undammed, the East River is a wild, winding river boasting huge, fishy bend pools, pocket water, riffles, and darkdeep cut banks creating epic trout fishing along its entire route with the four miles below the Roaring Judy Hatchery posted as Wild Trout Water. At Almont, the East converges with the Taylor River to form the fabled Gunnison River. Make sure to stop at the hatchery and walk around the long, skinny holding tanks. You'll see fry, fingerlings, and gigantic trout.

Reaching the East River's headwaters at Emerald Lake requires a gutsy drive up Gothic Road (FR 317) north of Crested Butte. At Snodgrass Mountain, the East flows away from the road, runs around Crested Butte Mountain, and converges with CO 135, skirting the road all the way to Almont. From Gunnison, travel north on CO 135. At Almont, take the left fork, continuing north on CO 135.

Barrett's hopper

Another option for small-stream fishing is the East Fork of Hermosa Creek, a feeder creek that, at first glance, doesn't look like much. Wrong. This winding meadow stream is easy and challenging, beautiful and maddening.

The East Fork, ten or twelve feet wide at its widest, is chock-full of fish. When it's running high, the creek spreads out over the meadow with its stands here and there of pine, patches of columbine, Parry's primrose, shrubby cinquefoil, and Indian paintbrush. You can fish a one-hundred-yard-long area for hours with every lie a bounty. Let all the other anglers drive across the East Fork to the parking lot and hike into big sister Hermosa Creek while you fish the pockets, cut banks, and bank pools of the little sister. You'll reach Hermosa Creek and the East Fork behind Durango Mountain Resort through a labyrinth of dirt roads (high clearance recommended).

This is great fly fishing water, packed with small, feisty, colorful brook trout and, in the upper reaches, Colorado cutthroats. This is also challenging angling, the water nearly opaque, the trout skittish, and the casting demanding. Undercut banks hide these brilliant but diminutive natives. The East Fork is a spring creek that snakes slowly across thick, grassy meadows and hilly slopes, through a canyon and back through a long meadow. Every now and again, you'll catch a twelve-inch cutthroat or a ten-inch brookie that makes you forget all the six-inch trout you've been catching. And the colors on these wild trout are Technicolor crazy. The start of fishing lies forty miles north of Durango. Take U.S. 550 north, then travel six miles west of Durango Mountain Resort on Hermosa Park Road (Forest Road 578), a route accessible by two-wheel-drive vehicles. The creek flows through a meadow below you and to the left. The road continues upstream and parallels the trailhead near the junction of East Fork and the main stem.

Royal trude

East Fork water is like one of those shimmery, sequined coats that Liberace wore. The water's color depends on the light: the water is cobalt under gray clouds, and then it's linen-gauzy-white in the bright light of noon, and then it's peach-puff and salmon against the big rocks, and finally, in the evening when the sun drops below the canyon walls, the East Fork becomes cadet and tranquil. The East Fork of the San Juan River lies north of Pagosa Springs in the San Juan Valley. Along the banks, you'll find ponderosa pine and Gambel oak.

Since the road follows the river so closely in the lower reaches, the East Fork has lots of angling and camping traffic so the best way to find solitude is to slide down a scree slope into the canyon. Get away from pullouts and campgrounds.

Get into the gorge. This is fun, fast, choppy-water fishing, best performed by high-sticking a dropper rig through all the pools and pockets. Rainbows and browns hiding behind rocks await your offering.

Get away from the crowds another way by taking the high roads. Drive north on main road and you'll have options to turn to fish the upper main stem or Quartz Creek. To reach the East Fork of the San Juan, drive north out of Pagosa Springs on U.S. 160 eleven miles and turn right on FR 667 (a.k.a. East Fork Road) for three-quarters of a mile where you'll have the campground for access. You can continue up the East Fork Road because it parallels the river for several miles on its way to and beyond the Continental Divide (four-wheel drive required beyond its junction with FR 684).

East Fork of the San Juan River

Rubber-legged foam hopper

A remote feeder to the West Fork of the Dolores River, Fish Creek is for small-stream enthusiasts who don't mind spending a day (or a few days) getting away from it all. You'll rarely see other anglers. The rainbows and browns are generally small but eager, ranging from about seven to ten inches but in deep pools and hard-to-reach hiding spots, it's not unusual to be surprised by a brown trout in the mid-teens. Six to ten feet wide, brushy in places, meadowy in others, Fish Creek is a wild joy. Wear long sleeves and bring insect repellent because the meadows are thick, wet, and full of mosquitoes.

North of Dolores, south of Telluride, you reach Fish Creek by taking CO 145 out of Dolores and turning on West Fork Dolores Road (FR 535). You'll see FR 736 at the confluence of Fish Creek and West Fork. Take that road past one mile of private land and back to the parking lot at Fish Creek State Wildlife Area. A marginal trail follows the creek up to its headwaters through ponderosa, scrub oak, and aspen stands.

Fish Creek

Yellow humpy

The Florida River is wet-wading heaven and a dry fly dreamland, fifteen minutes from Durango. The upper Florida flows rapidly down a steep canyon, slowed down by rocky pools, with water as clear as Grey Goose. The riverbed is chock-full of rocks of all colors, smoothed out and rounded. You'll need to wade and bushwhack because the thick ponderosa and the dense riparian habitat eat flies. Concentrate on the big pools, the rugged chutes, and the pocket water. As you fish up, you'll fish pool, drop, pool, drop, pool, plunge, flat, pool, and pocket water, and you'll be catching rainbows, browns, and brookies, most in the eight- to twelve-inch range.

You want to fish in solitude for wild trout? You want to cast dry flies in flat, glassy pools and shooting chutes? You fish the upper Florida River because you want to get away from it all—to fish with dries and enjoy the rugged cliffs, pristine freestone water, and thick forests of blue spruce, aspen, and Douglas fir. And if you want to fit in, pronounce the river's name correctly, Flo-ree-dah. An eight-foot, 4-weight outfit is ideal for the upper Florida.

From Durango, travel east on Florida Road (CR 240) twelve miles, then turn north on CR 243. You will shortly run into Lemon Reservoir and keep right on going to the north side of Lemon. A footpath follows the river on both sides.

Florida River

Mysis shrimp

Designated a Gold Medal Water, the forty-two-mile Fryingpan River is dammed near its midpoint, close to the town of Meredith, creating Ruedi Reservoir. Locals have dubbed the spillway just below Ruedi Dam the "Toilet Bowl," where trout gorge on mysis shrimp and reach average weights of four pounds and can grow up to fifteen pounds.

While some may think of breakfast upon hearing the words "frying pan," fly fishers think of mysis shrimp patterns, and midges in all shapes, colors, stages, and sizes. They also think *year-round tail water fishery*. Limestone walls contain "the Pan" below Ruedi, making for a fourteen-mile, fertile insect hatchery with as varied and prolific hatches as any tailrace in Colorado.

The Fryingpan below Ruedi Reservoir has 8.5 miles of public—though spotty—access east of Basalt along FR 105 (Fryingpan Road), with some favorite access points being at Strawberry Rock, the Fryingpan Valley welcome sign, Big Hat, Rosie's Pool, Baetis Bridge, and of course, the Toilet Bowl. Two of the photos accompanying this section were taken by two friends of ours, Sam Denham and Cylar Brown, who live close to the river and get to fish it on a regular basis. Yes, we are jealous.

In Basalt, take CO 82, turn at the Ruedi Reservoir sign, and follow the road 2.1 miles to a stop sign. Turn left at the sign onto Midland Avenue (which becomes Fryingpan Road) and go 28.6 miles to a campground sign. Bear right at the sign onto a dirt road and go 0.2 miles to the campground.

Fryingpan River

Hi-vis parachute Adams

Gore Creek

If you value wilderness and solitude, Gore Creek is not for you. You fish Gore Creek because you are staying in or around Vail. We're not diminishing the quality of the angling in this spry, fun creek, because you can certainly catch lots of fish, some of them worth bragging about. The value in Gore Creek is that while the kids are skiing or the wife is shopping, you can sneak out for an hour or an afternoon of fishing this clear, cold creek since it runs right through Vail. The creek runs through aspen, spruce, and Douglas fir forests.

Gore Creek feeds Eagle River near Minturn southwest of Vail. From the town of Vail to the confluence, Gore Creek has been designated as a Gold Medal Water, which means, though you are restricted to artificial flies and trout limits, the fishing is high quality. It's weird the first time fishing through the resort town, under the gaze of folks in condos and walking on a sidewalk, but after you have a few fat fish on the end of your line, you lose your self-consciousness.

One of the hidden treats of Gore is its upper section. From Gore Creek Campground upstream, the creek is frisky with the occasional cutthroat. At Vail, off Interstate 70, take Exit 180 (Vail east entrance) to the stop sign. Turn right onto Bighorn Road and go 2.3 miles to the campground sign. You can park past the sign. You can also access the river all through the resort town.

Rubber-legged orange Stimulator

The Gunnison River, from its clear mountain headwater stretches that are full of wild, colorful trout darting from pool to run, to the wide, flat pocket water south of the town of Gunnison, to the deep gorge and below, is a long-productive, diverse fishery, as diverse as any we know of in the Southwest. The Gunnison is designated a Gold Medal river. Think of the Gunnison and its seventy-five miles in three sections: the upper Gunnison from Almont, the Black Canyon of the Gunnison, and Gunnison Gorge.

The upper twenty miles of the river above the haunted landscape of Blue Mesa Reservoir is a mixture of public and private land, about half and half, usually well marked. With so many angling options around the upper Gunnison, with as much river as there is to fish, the fishing pressure is often light. Sure, in some stretches you'll see five anglers lined up in the middle of the river, tossing flies. You get good dry fly fishing on the main upper river and on its tributaries. Hatches of insects are heavy but unpredictable. June has a monster stonefly hatch, and July and August will find caddis and mayfly (blue-winged olives) hatches.

We like to fish the wide ranchland below Gunnison (when we can stand the mosquitoes). Willows and cottonwoods line the banks, and the trout are fat and sassy (rainbow, brown, and cutthroat). You'll find plenty of public access from Almont to Blue Mesa, and it's usually well marked. Consider a guide or a float trip to really fish it well. From Gunnison on U.S. 50, turn north on CO 135 (going toward Crested Butte), drive for approximately eleven miles, and you'll hit Almont and the start of the Gunnison.

Gunnison River

Doc's super caddis

There are rivers that you fall in love with despite the fact that they're not the best, the wildest, or the prettiest. So it goes with Henson Creek. Henson Creek is one of those wild and woolly western rivers that once you fish it, you are indebted to it for the fears it creates, for the perpetual primitiveness of the rocks and blue water, for the hits and misses, and for the numerous mines. The river is entirely too accessible. The one-time mining road follows the river curve for curve, but don't let that scare you off. Henson Creek is a canyon stream near Lake City, replete with scree slopes, sentinel boulders, and steep canyon walls. Engineer Pass Road follows aspen and pine trees along Henson Creek up to the pass.

As you stand on the road's edge peering over into the river, you see swirling, foamy aqua heads of pools that carved out of these granite walls, deep enough water to make you fear falling in, so deep that below what you can see is a scary filter of cloudy ink water.

Henson Creek fish are often heavy, girthy, and brightly colored—so much of the color green in the rainbow trout. Most take caddis off the water, making brilliant swirls in pocket water.

Park in a pullout and walk upstream and fish from the road. When you want, slide down into the canyon and climb huge rocks. You can walk or drive upstream for miles and miles. You'll find that there's always a picture-perfect stretch just around the bend. Wading can be dicey because of the tricky waters, the climbing over boulders, the steepness down into the canyon. You won't find spots in these pools and pockets where you need a lot of classic casting—bring out your bag of short-lining, flips, dapping, and high-sticking. Dry-dropper rigs work great.

From Lake City, turn west onto Second Street. Drive 0.1 miles and turn left onto Henson Creek Road. This is the Alpine Loop Scenic Byway. You have about 12 miles of two-wheel-drive pullouts and clearly marked public/private access. After that, you'll need four-wheel drive.

Henson Creek

Winged black foam ant

"Hermosa" means "beautiful" in Spanish and the name-sake stream is true to its moniker. This tributary to the Animas River, "located north of Durango behind Durango Mountain Ski Resort, is tailor-made for dry fly enthusiasts. Hermosa Creek runs through meadows covered in wildflowers and through a wooded canyon, past aspen, blue spruce, ponderosa pine, southwestern white pine, and Gambel oak. The river's cold, transparent waters course through true wilderness. The stream is full of pocket water and pools teeming with eager brook, brown, and rainbow trout.

It's a decent little hike from the parking lot back into lower Hermosa but nothing we'd call strenuous. The up-and-down trail is hard-packed, not especially crowded but not sweet solitude, either. You are far from the river, then up above the river looking down, then riverside. Watch for lots of columbines on both sides of the trail—great photo ops. And the fishing is so much better the farther you walk.

Hermosa Creek is drop-dead gorgeous. The water gurgles and percolates around gray-white rocks, dumps and drops into plunge pools, slashes beneath cut banks, wiggles and riffles, dances and dips. Dry fly nirvana.

The trout are bigger than they ought to be in a stream this size. From time to time, lucky anglers land a trout that is eighteen inches, legit. The average rainbow and cutbow you'll catch will be in the ten- to fourteen-inch range, and while the brookies aren't that big, they will be fat and bigger than you expect. Hermosa trout rise willingly to dry flies, hatch or not. Just get a good presentation, decent drift over new water, and you'll get a strike. Waders beware: the rocks are slippery greased bowling balls.

Take U.S. 550 north, then go six miles west of Durango Mountain Resort on the Hermosa Park Road (Forest Road 578), accessible by two-wheel drive. You'll see the East Fork of Hermosa Creek flowing through a meadow below you and to the left. The road continues upstream and parallel to the trailhead near the junction of East Fork and the main stem. From here, you walk into Hermosa Creek, an easy one-mile hike.

Hermosa Creek

Orange humpy

This is a bubbly Animas feeder creek that's a great early season or fall choice. This in-town Durango creek is no secret, but the crowds typically aren't other anglers. They are joggers and hikers and kids and dogs on the trail that runs through the ponderosa pine, fir, and Gambel oak forest (with a smattering of cottonwoods). There are also trout—brook and rainbow. The brook trout are small and as colorful as a painter's palette. The rainbows are tremendously spotted, rich with purples and reds. Be prepared to have the kids or dogs jump in your pool. Annoying, to be sure, but that's part of the utility of this stream. It's not often you find a great little getaway right in the middle of town.

A trail (part of the Colorado Trail) follows the stream from the parking lot for 2.5 miles to a bridge. Fishing gets tougher the farther you walk, but the payoff is that the higher stretches are much less fished than the lower stretches. If you can get a fly on the water from the middle section up, you'll have a strike.

Junction Creek is reached by a west turn at 25th Street off of U.S. 550 as you head north through Durango. Travel 2.9 miles and stay left at the "Y" (you'll see a sign pointing you to Junction Creek). Note that 25th Street changes to Junction Street, then CR 204. In 2.1 miles, you will reach the first of two trailhead choices where the pavement ends and FR 171 begins. You can park in the lot to your left. One mile farther, at the Junction Creek Campground area, there is a second parking area and another access point.

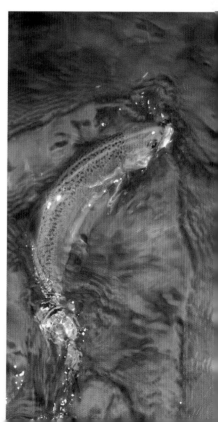

Rubber-legged copper john

Above La Jara Reservoir, the La Jara Creek headwaters remain dry in all but the wettest of years. But below the dam, La Jara Creek flows year-round, coursing through a gorgeous high meadow and cascading down a series of falls a few miles below.

Hiking into La Jara Canyon below RD 249 offers a fly fishing experience in some of southern Colorado's most unvisited and unknown brown trout waters. With rocky pockets, serpentine slicks, and lengthy riffles, La Jara Creek demands its anglers be fit and athletic—and own a full repertoire of casts and strategies.

Above the La Jarosa Creek union exists exceptional trout fishing. But downstream, where a spring bubbles into La Jara Creek from the west, is even better. Between the shadows of two ten-thousand-foot mesas, anglers have a superb opportunity to land large browns on dry flies. But because of a short season, poor road conditions (the rough road can get muddy quickly), and extremely remote, limited access, this isn't for the faint of heart. Fish at your own risk in this wild country, since there's not much in the way of stores or services nearby.

From Antonito, take U.S. 285 south 0.3 miles to CO 17. Continue west on CO 17 35.2 miles to the Trujillo Meadows Reservoir sign. Turn right onto the dirt road at the sign and go 0.1 miles to a "T" intersection and campground sign (FR 118). Turn right on FR 118 and go 2.1 miles to a campground on the right.

La Jara Creek

Beadhead hare's ear nymph

Located west of Durango near Hesperus, the La Plata is one of those unexpected joys you occasionally find after passing it up for years. You won't catch large trout in this mountain stream, and you'll have to slog through tight trails and scramble over loose rocks to fish it. The payoff for this fast, clear, cold stream is that few others fish it. Fair fishing, great scenery, and solitude are a great combination any time. A great day-trip from Durango.

Don't even think about fishing below the so-called town of Mayday. The mine has tainted all the water below it. Concentrate on the water above, especially the dancing waters around and above Snowslide and Kroeger Campgrounds. The river runs past large spruce and Douglas fir stands dotted with some aspens and cottonwoods. Work the riffles and pocket water with attractor dry flies, and you'll be surprised by the colorful rainbow and brook trout (and in the lower reaches, brown trout). Run a nymph through the plunge pools and you will be rewarded. Use high-stick methods, wet wade or wear hip waders, use seven-foot rods, and lastly, make this your secret super fall getaway.

Take U.S. 160 west from Durango. After about nine miles, you will turn north onto CR 124 (that later turns into FR 498). If you keep going up, know that the road becomes a rough four-wheel-drive passage on its way to Kennebec Pass.

La Plata River

Ribbed hare's ear beadhead

A lesser-known Wild Trout Water, as designated by the Colorado Division of Wildlife, the headwaters of the Lake Fork of the Conejos begin at over twelve thousand feet above sea level. Here, the stream is a small yet productive rivulet full of palm-sized brook trout and some Rio Grande cutthroats. The downstream stretches between Big Lake and Rock Lake cultivate large, wild trout thriving in a multitude of wine-dark pools overlooked by sentinel aspens and mixed conifers.

We have both hiked up Lake Fork and found it wild and worthwhile. From Lake Fork Campsite on FR 250, a stream-side trail sticks close to the low rushing of the water upon the rocks. Fish-hiking upstream is intense and will offer unmatched photo ops.

Backpacking higher, between Mammoth Mountain (11,385 feet) and Conejos Peak (12,600 feet), is nothing short of spectacular, but not for the inexperienced. Be prepared for mosquitoes and Klondike-cold temperatures, even in summer, and bring along an army of dry flies and nymphs for the lakes as well. Think chironomids.

From Antonito, take U.S. 285 south 0.3 miles to CO 17. Continue on CO 17 and go 21.9 miles to the Platoro sign (FR 250). Turn right at the sign onto Road 250 (dirt) and go 17.5 miles to a campground sign. Turn left into the campground or park nearby.

Lake Fork of the Conejos

Kaufmann's stonefly nymph

The Lake Fork of the Gunnison, near Lake City, is a medium-sized, rugged canyon river, with roadside access to nearly sixteen public miles of a thirty-one-mile course below Lake San Cristobal. The Lake Fork flows north out from Lake City and ends up dumping into Blue Mesa Reservoir. From its American Basin headwaters, the Lake Fork courses through high meadows and alternating spruce and aspen canyons, then tumbles out of the lake and picks up feeder streams, building volume and carving bigger and bigger pools. The Lake Fork offers anglers a dizzying array of ideal trout lies, choppy riffles and long runs, spotted with big, deep pools and inaccessible churning whitewater tucked tight between narrow canyon walls. This is an incredibly beautiful river.

There are four species of trout in the Lake Fork and its tributaries: cutthroat, rainbow, brown, and brook trout. Rainbows and browns are the predominant fish in the lower stem and every now and again reach twenty inches. Your usual hookup will find fat, feisty trout averaging about twelve to fourteen inches long.

The upper Lake Fork provides some of the prettiest scenery in Colorado, as well as consistent angling in its run-pool-riffle configurations. Anglers can enjoy another sixteen miles of access above the spectacular natural lake caused by the collapse of a mountain (the Slumgullion Slide), which dammed the Lake Fork River several hundred years ago.

The upper reaches of the Lake Fork of the Gunnison can be accessed from either Cinnamon Pass (from Silverton) or from Lake City, as Cinnamon Pass Road (CR 30) parallels most of the river's course. The lower Lake Fork of the Gunnison runs beside CO 149 as the river flows north to its confluence with Blue Mesa Reservoir and the Gunnison River. At Gateview, CO 149 turns east, so take 64 RD north to follow the river into Sapinero Canyon or CR 25 northwest to reach the Gateview and Red Bridge sections.

Lake Fork of the Gunnison

Rubber-legged Stimulator

Lime Creek is one of the finest streams in southern Colorado. The cold water is as clear as plate glass, the multicolored cobbled bottom is ideal for hiding colorful brook trout, and the stream is loaded with runs, flats, pocket water, and pools. Lime is perfect for beginning anglers, and we often take rookies here to learn how to fly fish.

The brook trout are small. They are wild, brightly colored, eager, and numerous. If you're halfway decent, you'll catch great numbers of these. Don't drive the rough road back into Lime just for the great numbers of brook trout.

Don't hike Purgatory Trail to fish Lime just for the fishing. Lime Creek is an experience, a contract with wilderness. Aspen, spruce, and pine forests snuggle up to the cold creek.

We recommend a four-wheel-drive vehicle, but it's not always necessary because we see two-wheel-drive vehicles parked along the stream all the time. From Durango, travel north on U.S. 550 for thirty miles. Go past the turnoff for Purgatory Ski Area. Turn east onto Old Lime Creek Road (FR 591). The road rejoins U.S. 550 twelve miles later.

Lime Creek

Royal Wulff

The falls alone are worth a trip to this Rio Grande feeder stream. It's weird, too. North Clear Creek, at an elevation of ten thousand feet, runs across a wide, flat, grassy, treeless valley floor that is winding and shallow, only to find a chasm, some one-hundred-feet deep. North Clear Creek Falls drops to the boulder-strewn canyon floor. Below the falls, the river flows through a canyon with all the requisite pocket water and boulder-pocked pools until it emerges and flows across a wide and sometimes brushy park.

The stream fishes like two different rivers. Above the falls up to Continental Reservoir, you'll find deep water, deep bend pools, wide runs, and cut banks. Below the falls, the creek adds feeders on its way to the Rio Grande as it flows past thick spruce and some aspen trees and heavy riparian habitat in the park. North Clear Creek holds cutthroat, rainbow, cutbow, and brook trout. The rainbows below the falls are fat and as athletic as any you'll ever catch.

From Creede, take CO 149 south (toward Lake City) 21.6 miles to North Clear Creek Road sign (Forest Road 510). Turn right at the sign onto FR 510 (gravel) and go 2.1 miles to the campground sign. Turn right into the campground. From the three campgrounds along the stream (South Clear Creek Campground, North Clear Creek Campground, and South Clear Creek Falls Campground) you can set up, or you can drive easily from Lake City, too (about halfway between there and Creede).

North Clear Creek

Elk hair caddis

Named for the willows networking their way up this tiny tributary, Osier Creek is tough fishing in places, barely visible through the cover in others, but well worth the out-of-the-way drive to get there. The Osier train station, still in use today, sits on rusty, coal-laden tracks overlooking Osier Creek where it connects with Rio de los Pinos, harkening back to the era when people and product were shipped, even through the most difficult terrain, by rail. We suggest stopping and eating a bite in the restaurant before hiking upstream.

Once at streamside, Osier fishes like any other brushy headwater; water clarity is like the vodka in your flask, pools are key locations to drop dry flies, and fish are as wily as coyotes in daylight. But believe us when we say there are large trout hiding beneath the surface. One time one of us caught, fought, and netted a brown trout (unexpectedly) that reached every bit of fourteen inches. The other was fishing the Pinos, fifty yards away, and missed all the action. Feeding on relentless swarms of hoppers, Osier fish reach "oddity" proportions.

From CO 17, find FR 103 near the gauging station downstream from Fox Creek on the Conejos River, following this scenic road for approximately twelve miles to the train station. Take your hoppers and some water and start at the confluence, fishing upstream as far as your legs will allow.

Floatzilla

$\mathcal{A}$ Rio Grande feeder stream, this jaunty creek is one of our favorite sleepers in southern Colorado. Park Creek is one of those streams you pass by every time, but as you pass, you look and think to yourself, *one of these days, I'd like to fish that.* Do it.

What's to like about Park Creek? The upper meadow section is a lazy, clear, long run that winds back and forth and holds some trout bigger than you'd think. The middle stretches are choppy, rife with riffles, ideal for dry flies, and thick with understory and heavy spruce forest. The lower part dives and plunges past boulders the size of ice coolers forming fecund pools and chutes. The upper section is supposed to hold cutthroats, but all we have ever caught are browns (the predominant fish in Park Creek) and brookies.

The creek does get what some might call heavy pressure because of primitive campsites along the river and the highway traffic, but here's what we find: most anglers stick close to camp or close to easy access. If you have an adventurous spirit or like to climb and wade, you can find all kinds of spots that few will fish. Avoid one mistake some make— don't fish just dries. Add a short dropper with a beadhead nymph because these browns don't tend to feed up top.

FR 380 off of U.S. 160 parallels the stream to Summit Pass. In South Fork, at the intersection of CO 149 and U.S. 160, take U.S. 160 west 7.8 miles to the Park Creek Campground sign. Turn left at the sign into the campground, and the road follows the creek.

Park Creek

Yellow Stimulator

You won't find Pass Creek in any other fishing guidebooks. It's a drive-by creek for everyone else. Park. Fish. Enjoy.

Between Pagosa Springs and South Fork on the north side of Wolf Creek Pass, Pass Creek (hence its name) flows beside U.S. 160. The creek enters the South Fork of the Rio Grande at the junction of U.S. 160 and FR 410. Pass Creek is deep blue, choppy, and pooly. Boulders the size of Airstreams line the banks. It's all you want in a stream, but anglers drive right past it to get somewhere else. Go figure.

Forests line the banks—Englemann spruce, ponderosa pine, Douglas fir, and Colorado blue spruce.

We've caught trout as long as twenty inches here. We've lost some bigger. One we won't forget. For the most part, you'll catch trout in the ten- to fourteen-inch range. We catch mostly rainbows and cutbows but we've talked to a couple of others who like this stream who catch mostly cutthroats and brookies.

You have a few riffles, but mostly it's big pocket water and bigger pools. Park along the road in a pullout and fish from the big rocks for a while, but sooner or later, you're gonna have to get out and wade upstream. Get ready for a treat. Stick with a 4- or 5-weight because of the big water and heavy trout.

From South Fork, travel west on U.S. 160 for six miles. Just south of the turnoff for Big Meadow Campground, Pass Creek enters the South Fork of the Rio Grande. Drive past that road, and you have several miles up to and past Tucker Ponds to fish. Parking pullouts are few, so grab the first one you see.

Red ant

High in the Saguache Wilderness, south of Gunnison, way back on what seem to be eternal dirt roads, Pauline Creek crosses at a hairpin turn. A short, step-across, serpentine liquefaction full of bend pools and cut banks—as well as wild brown trout, rainbow trout, and in the higher reaches, Colorado cutthroat—this little gem is worth the drive up from Cochetopa Creek. Narrow and winding, Pauline requires both stealth and accuracy. To fish it well, stand way back, walk very softly and be willing to cast from your knees. Use long, thin leaders.

One might encounter any number of wildlife on the way to Pauline (we did several times), but rest assured, once a dry fly or beadhead breaks the surface, so will a trout. To reach Pauline, you'll want to use Cochetopa as your home base. From Dome Lakes, take 15 GG Road southwest to 14 DD Road. It's a short drive to FR 794, a dirt road. Drive about 2.5 miles until you reach Pauline Creek.

Guy's fly hopper

Located northeast of Durango, the Pine River is an excellent backpacking or horse-packing destination. What hurts is, as you drive up the Pine River Valley, looking at the amazing stream flowing through it, you can't fish it. Not this lower part below Vallecito Reservoir. All private.

So you get to fish the upper Pine (a.k.a. Los Pinos River). Nothing wrong with it. The hike in is long, the fish are wild, and the scenery is spectacular. You can hike in three to four miles—it's not an easy hike either—and hike back out, but that's a mighty long day. Think about backpacking for a night or two. Mixed conifers, aspens, and ponderosa pines stay tight to the trail and the canyon, sheltering the streamside trail.

You'll catch rainbows, brooks, and cutthroats with some browns. Most of the trout will run about eight to twelve inches, and they're plentiful. But weirdly, in some spots you won't catch but one, and it'll be a large one (thirteen to sixteen inches). All of the upper Pine restricts anglers to artificial flies and bag limits.

We'll give Bayfield directions because one of the authors has a cabin in Pine Valley—drive north from U.S. 160 on CR 501. Drive a little over eight miles and head north (don't turn left at the junction) on what becomes CR 240. CR 240 will take you to Vallecito Reservoir where you'll follow the west side of the lake till you reach FR 602. Stay right till you reach the trailhead at Pine River Campground. Angling is limited to flies and lures, and there is a bag and possession limit of two fish.

Pine River (Los Pinos)

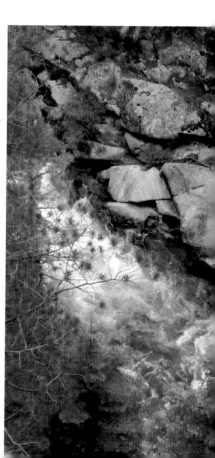

Royal Gorgeous

The Piedra River is a canyon river, east of Durango, west and north of Pagosa Springs, loaded with fat browns and foot-long rainbows swimming in its forty miles of pocket water and deep pools. The Piedra flows through isolated granite box canyons in some of the wildest country in the West.

Think rocks ("piedra" in Spanish means "rock"). Lots of big rocks. And rocks mean stoneflies. Lots of stoneflies. The Piedra muddies quickly, but if you are on it when it is clear, you should expect some of the best stonefly hatches in the state. But the key to success on the Piedra is to fish every likely lie and to make sure to nymph the pocket water. Dries will work a lot of the time, but these trout love to take their food under the surface.

You're not likely to encounter other fishers along the medium-size stream. The Piedra is in wild country, very little of which is accessible by vehicle. Anglers should expect to hike a bit to get to the Piedra's deep holes and glassy pockets.

This is an incredible place to hike in, camp out, and catch a lot of wild trout.

To get to the lower Piedra, travel west from Pagosa Springs twenty miles on U.S. 160 where the river crosses the road (at Piedra). Turn north on FR 622. The road follows the river, more or less, for ten miles. There is a parking area at the trailhead. Largely a hike-in stream, the Piedra has two gravel-road accesses from both the east and west sides at this southern end. The eastside road runs upstream for ten miles along ponderosa pine forest.

Several trails reach the river from the road. To reach the upper Piedra, drive north from Pagosa Springs on Piedra River Road. The road turns into FR 631. Stay on it for more than seventeen miles until you cross a bridge. After crossing the bridge, there is a parking area and trailhead on the left. Walk and wade carefully. You're a long way from a hospital.

Pale morning dun

Although many believe in a dark, religious place called Purgatory, a state of punishment and purification for the dead before ascending to Heaven, there is little reason to fear the French-spelled Purgatoire River in southern Colorado. Locally termed the "Picketwire," the river is surrounded by recreation, bound by scenery, and rich in geologic history. The Purgatoire River is located near the old mining community of Cuchara on the Scenic Highway of Legends in southern Colorado.

The brushy headwaters above Weston are fertile and fun, with the West and North Forks holding small brookies, browns in the ten- to twelve-inch range, and feisty cutthroats slashing out to take dry flies in fast water. We fished this area with McPhail's kids, Wesley and Savannah, when they were only six and eight. Even at those ages, with imperfect casts and sketchy drifts, they each tied into teams of wild trout, learning fly fishing basics along these tributaries' banks.

We've fished the Cuchara area for decades but love the Purgatoire best of all of the area's waters. While you're there, check out the geography. The dikes or walls you'll find throughout the area rise up like one hundred Spinosaurus. Crustal fracturing formed more than five hundred of these walls in the Raton Basin.

From La Veta, take CO 12 south 25.3 miles to a campground sign (FR 34). Turn right at the sign onto FR 34 (gravel) and go 0.2 miles to the "T" intersection. Turn right, and voilà, the river runs beside the road for several miles.

Purgatoire River

Gray Wulff

Flowing southeast and interlacing the Colorado–New Mexico border, Rio de los Pinos originates at an elevation of nearly twelve thousand feet in the South San Juan Wilderness. McPhail caught his first Rio Grande cutthroat here, catapulting a love affair with wild, backcountry trout.

The upper river is punctuated by falls, pools, bends, and fast-running riffles. Wild browns, brookies, and Rio Grande cutthroats thrive on a multitude of insects, but these trout will zap nearly any fly at any time.

The stream below Trujillo Meadows Reservoir State Wildlife Area is dominated by larger water, steep canyon walls, and sizeable rainbows and browns as well (although the numbers seemed down the past few years). The historic Cumbres & Toltec Scenic Railroad skirts the stream, where two designated Wild Trout Waters, Cascade Creek and Osier Creek, add to the streamflow and the wild trout experience. Hiking an hour or two up each can make the entire trip worthwhile.

Find the campground at Trujillo Meadows by traveling west out of Antonito on CO 17 and turning back west on FR 118 just before entering Cumbres Pass. It's easy to get lost in the backcountry because nothing is marked well. If you turn and come to a yurt-like house, as we have twice, turn around. And get a good map or GPS.

Rio de los Pinos

Hare's ear beadhead

The nation's second-longest river, the storied Rio Grande runs through beautiful and rugged southwestern Colorado country, where it begins its southward trek. The river swells with tributary after tributary, surrounded by interconnecting trails and alpine lakes. The water is as clear as air, the surrounding green mountains are majestic, and the trout are plentiful. The river holds some whoppers.

So you have a freestone stream in a wilderness setting with numerous tributaries. Deep runs, big pools, riffles, all kinds of water flowing through narrow canyons and broad valleys. You're in some of the most primeval scenery left in the lower forty-eight states. One of the great things about this upper section of the Rio Grande is that despite its remoteness and lack of angling pressure, the river is easily accessed by road and trail. The Rio Grande is a big river by southern Colorado standards, but if you treat it like a small river, you'll do better. Look for holding spots behind big boulders—try cut banks and seams and runs and riffles. Work a section instead of getting intimidated by the size of the water. Watch for hatches, especially caddis and green drake, and change your fly and alter your nymph level.

The river holds brown, rainbow, and some cutthroat and brook trout. The rainbows average ten to fourteen inches and the browns twelve to fifteen inches, and you'll have the opportunity to land some much longer and heavier.

The beauty of the Rio Grande as it collects in the rugged San Juan Mountains may be unparalleled by any other western river. This is wild country defined by dense forests, stunning mountain vistas, and steep, dark canyons. Fishing from a raft is a great choice for anglers. In the middle to lower reaches, say by Palisade Campground, you get hit with frolicking, noisy rafters slowly floating past cottonwoods and a wide, open valley. At Palisades, also watch for eagles in the air and bighorn sheep on the cliffs.

The Rio Grande is located in southwestern Colorado near Creede and South Fork. U.S. 160 parallels the river before Del Norte, up to South Fork. From South Fork upstream, CO 149 follows the river to Creede. Anglers will find plenty of well-marked public accesses and pullouts along the river, but there is a mix of private and public water, so pay attention.

Wilcox's para variant

The Roaring Fork, especially around Basalt, flows as a classic, clear-water, freestone stream, wearing many masks as it rushes seventy miles through the Centennial State. Dropping more than 4,200 feet in elevation in that distance, the Roaring Fork offers sleek, shallow, easily waded sections, separated by gouging whitewater chutes and rapids along its entire length. Aspens, cottonwoods, and some mixed conifers line the banks. The land is heavy with wild roses, grass, wildflowers, and shrubs. There's some big fish in this water, and they don't come to the net without a fight.

Anglers fishing various sections of "the Fork" (as those who fish it often refer to it) get a twofer: Colorado's prestigious stamps of Gold Medal Water and Wild Trout Water. In summer, flies such as green drakes and salmon flies produce crashing strikes from browns and bows, and midge patterns dupe fish throughout the dead of winter. Most anglers concentrate on the waters from Aspen to Interstate 70, but we don't want you to overlook the headwaters above Aspen. Headwatering southeast of Aspen, the Fork is extremely accessible all along CO 82, fishing well through the towns of Aspen and Basalt (where the Fryingpan spills in), northwesterly to Carbondale, and then on to Glenwood Springs.

Peacock humpy Wulff

From the crazy traffic of rafters, waders, and kayakers in the middle of Pagosa Springs, to the solitude of the West Fork, the San Juan River is a classic western backcountry stream, as well as an amazing water resource for anglers (and recreationalists).

Let's start in town. The San Juan River runs through it. Through good management, these few miles are pretty darned good water now. For one, you're in town. Two, you can fish while the family plays. Three, anywhere you are in town, you can access the river. Four, the river is fishable all year long. And five? They stock really big fish in town. North of Pagosa Springs, the upper forks of the San Juan run through canyons and valleys. The West Fork is less accessible and the East Fork has too much access.

The West Fork is probably one of the prettiest rivers in all of southern Colorado. Twenty minutes north of Pagosa Springs, you'll find the West Fork of the San Juan. This canyon-meadow stream has deep runs, wide flats and riffles, and bottomless green pools. What it doesn't have is large trout. There are lots of trout, rainbows and cutthroats, browns and brookies, ten to twelve inches long (with the occasional mid-teens), but you're hiking three miles into the river for the scenery and wilderness. Drive U.S. 160 from Pagosa Springs to West Fork Road (FR 648), turning north. Follow it to the West Fork Campground. Continue to the end of the road to the trailhead. This can be a rough road at times. From the trailhead at the end of road, hike upstream about three miles.

San Juan River

Yellow humpy

One of the great underrated trout streams in the Southwest, the San Miguel River is scenic, close to a great mountain town, and a blast to fish. Undammed and untamed, the San Miguel is full of personality and verve. At first glance, the San Miguel looks like a river made up of all riffles and fast water, but if you're patient and observant, you'll find the slow runs and deeper pools. If you do, you'll have a better chance to tie into the bigger rainbows and browns. That said, the trout don't tend to grow large, but they are full-bodied and athletic.

This lovely mountain stream flows past Jurassic and Triassic red sandstone canyon walls. More than fifty miles of the San Miguel hold excellent trout fishing in terrain ranging from high desert to alpine. Access to the main river or its forks is not a problem since roads generally parallel the drainage. Dry fly anglers adore this river. Fly fishers of all ages and skill levels will love that not only is the San Miguel a consistent producer but is also fishable all year long. Dropper rigs with

some kind of lightly weighted nymph work well and are the usual technique on the San Miguel. To reach the river, follow CO 145 west out of Telluride; the river follows the highway.

The riverine system holds willows and box elders, quaking aspens, bitter cress, and a variety of sedges. Colorado blue spruce, narrowleaf cottonwood, Douglas fir, thinleaf alder, water birch, and red osier dogwood also grace the banks of the river. In addition, you can find old-growth ponderosa pine in places along its course.

The San Miguel has two notable feeder streams: the Lake Fork and the South Fork. The Lake Fork of the San Miguel is a small river that begins under the gaze of one of the most recognized natural landmarks of southwestern Colorado, Lizard Head Peak. The Lake Fork parallels CO 145 after it leaves Trout Lake. FR 626 off of CO 145 can take you to the upper reaches of this brushy stream. The South Fork of the San Miguel is a sleeper stream that is not crowded, and the trout aren't selective.

San Miguel River

Lime Wulff

When traveling CO 145 to Rico and Telluride, we find a pullout along a crystal-clear stream tumbling adjacent to the road through Lizard Head Pass in easternmost Dolores County. Surrounded by Lizard Head Peak, Yellow Mountain, and Sheep Mountain, water sedge and thickets of wolf willow dominate the meadow through which Snow Spur Creek flows—the perfect cover for wily cutthroats, brookies, and browns to grow to surprising proportions for such a diminutive stream.

The rich riparian growth offers stealthy approaches and the same cover for us to ambush unsuspecting trout in Snow Spur's small pools and plunges. Within minutes, McPhail uses a Madam X trailed by a weighted hare's ear nymph to snare a twelve-inch brown dapping in an upstream pool. In the same time frame, Williams strikes it rich on the edges and riffles, landing three cutthroats bursting with colors. Snow Spur taught us to never underestimate small streams; some of our favorites are overlooked roadside runnels others pass by. To find Snowspur Creek, travel thirty-three miles to Rico from Telluride on CO 145 and go another four miles south of Rico.

Snow Spur Creek

Kaufmann's Stonefly nymph

We're so glad this Rio Grande feeder creek isn't well marked or well known. It's a gem. Beautiful, wild, and fishy.

One day, a few years back, we were on the creek fishing the usual dropper-dry combo, catching the usual average-size brooks and rainbows, when we tried a big salmon-fly pattern, more as a lark than an intention. The fat fly splatted next to an undercut bank and bam! A fat brown, nineteen inches long. We had no idea the stream held trout that big. The rest of the day, we tossed big stone dries at the cut banks and caught browns sixteen to twenty-two inches long. We haven't been able to duplicate it since. But South Clear Creek is a solid producer in a scenic canyon, and few others fish this medium-sized river.

Think day-trip from Creede or Lake City. Take CO 149 north from Creede. When you get close to FR 520 (where you turn off to go to Road Canyon Reservoir), look to your right for a dirt road that goes up a hill. If you get to the turn-off for the upper Rio Grande, go back and find that unmarked dirt road. You'll find a weathered Bureau of Land Management sign—go past it (in a high-clearance vehicle because the road is bad) and drive over the hill and park. Hike down to the river.

That's our way to get into South Clear Creek. Here's another way: from Creede, take CO 149 south (toward Lake City) 21.6 miles to the North Clear Creek Road sign (FR 510). Turn right at the sign onto FR 510 (gravel) and go 0.3 miles to a campground sign. Turn right at the sign into campground. The campground stretches 0.6 miles above South Clear Creek. Looming mountains watch over the stream. Spruce and aspens line the meadow and provide shade.

South Clear Creek

Idylwild's green drake parachute

Beautiful water . . . so good it looks like the forest gods designed their own trout stream with spectacular cliffs, dashing drops, foam-green runs, and Scylla and Charybdis pools. But for us, over the years, the Rio Grande's South Fork has been hit or miss.

U.S. 160 generally parallels the river's course to its confluence with the Rio Grande; a variety of conifers and aspens stand sentinel. The smaller stream above Big Meadows Reservoir and the tail water below it are our favorite stretches of the river (think fat cutthroats). We've fished the wide flats near the town of South Fork in late summer when the water ran warm and the fishing cold. We've caught lots of fish—some big fish—and had days where it had to be fine just to

have spent time on the water. The South Fork of the Rio Grande is fickle.

Some parts of the river have in-stream rehabilitation (weirs), a testament to the amount of angler traffic on the river. For us, the South Fork of the Rio Grande is a get-out-of-the-car-for-a-couple-of-hours kind of river or the kind of river you fish as one of your numerous options if you're staying in or around South Fork. Avoid the water close to Fun Valley, a sprawling monster of a campground south of town. In South Fork, at the intersection of CO 149 and U.S. 160, take U.S. 160 west 11.6 miles to the Big Meadows Reservoir sign. Turn right at the sign and go 1.4 miles to a "Y" intersection (FR 410).

South Fork of the Rio Grande

Yellow sally beadhead nymph

Linking Colorado's Mosquito Range and Antero Reservoir to the eastern side of South Park, the South Fork of the South Platte River undulates through an expansive intermontane grassland basin, bringing with it countless opportunities for trophy trout seekers with dry flies. Coursing between U.S. 285 and CO 9, anglers casting to riffles, grassy drop-offs, and seemingly bottomless pools will be unobstructed by pines, as well as people.

Upstream of Antero Reservoir, the South Fork is a freestone mountain stream containing wild—though petite—trout. But between Antero Dam and the town of Hartsel, where the Platte's South and Middle Forks converge, the South Fork earns its epic reputation. Here, terrestrials and tricos are a hit in summer and fall, while tiny midge patterns are a fine choice most of the year. The sections above and below the CO 9 and U.S. 24 intersection are favorite stopping points for many dry fly enthusiasts. Find a vacant pull-out and let it rip.

South Fork of the South Platte

Copper john

During your trip to fish for gargantuan trout on the Taylor River tail water, consider spending an afternoon (or a day) on charming Spring Creek. We've fished it a lot but also relied on fellow angler and Spring Creek expert Cylar Brown for the inside skinny. You can catch four different trout: brook, rainbow, cutthroat, and brown. Some of them grow large, larger than a medium-sized stream ought to hold. The creek gets decent pressure low and high, but there's so much delightful water (eleven miles worth), you won't have any problem finding your own area.

The fishable part of Spring Creek begins below Spring Creek Reservoir at high elevation. You get classic Colorado alpine stream configuration: high up, you get meadows; middle, you get canyon; lower, you get pocket water. The trout tend to be athletic fighters—shy, and pickier than you'd expect, reliant on the impressive hatches of mayfly and caddis. Stay back, stay low, use thin leaders, change flies to match the hatch, and change fly size. You'll have a field day on what is one of our favorite streams while being shaded by mixed conifers and aspens.

Located northeast of Gunnison and southeast of Crested Butte, Spring Creek is reached by driving north on CO 135 from Gunnison. Take a right at the fishing town of Almont (good fly shops and guides here). Drive north on Taylor Road for 6.5 miles until you reach Harmel's Resort. You'll see the Spring Creek turnoff.

Spring Creek

M & M midge pupa

The spectacular fishery of the South Platte River runs from Hartsel all the way to the Denver metro area. A short section of the river between Spinney Mountain and Eleven Mile Reservoirs is nicknamed "the Dream Stream" for obvious reasons. Also dubbed "Spinney Mile," it's easily fished, all 5.5 miles are public, and browns, rainbows, and Snake River cutthroats reach lengths of twenty-four inches and up. Come with your PhD hat on because these are trained, tricky fish, big and wary, conditioned to lots of turndowns of small flies. And the wind can be as difficult as the trout.

Aside from occasional gusty South Park winds and subfreezing temperatures in winter, there are few obstacles keeping trophy trout hunters from scooping heavy bounties into their nets on this or any other section of the South Platte, except other eager anglers and a challenging hike. Cheesman Canyon is another supreme section, as are Eleven Mile Canyon, the section near Deckers, and the tail water of Waterton Canyon. Each of these sections, barring the last, has potential to produce rod-shattering trout. Deciding where to fish first, however, will be your most challenging decision.

South Platte River

Lime copper john

Tarryall, meaning "a place to stay a while," was named by early placer miners in love with the gold they were finding in it. Tarryall Creek was one of the most active mining locations in the Colorado Gold Rush of 1859, and with the distinctions of being just a stone's throw away from the "Dream Stream" near Hartsel and boasting the label of Wild Trout Water, Tarryall Creek deserves its moniker.

The last two miles of Tarryall Creek, before it merges with the South Platte, earn its Wild Trout Water designation, but every inch of this stream is productive, classic Colorado trout-fishing water, bearing multifaceted characteristics and lots of trout. Finding well-marked public access will be the toughest part of the day.

Reachable from either U.S. 285 from the north or U.S. 24 from the south, 77 RD follows Tarryall Creek's entire length, except the last few miles, where a four-wheel drive and strong legs will get you to the best canyon stretches of the stream.

Tarryall Creek

Dirk's epoxy mysis shrimp

A constant conveyor belt of mysis shrimp spews from the turbines below Taylor Reservoir, creating a never-ending food supply for the trout waiting in the tail water downstream. Like whales engulfing plankton, eager rainbows and browns engorge themselves on astronomical numbers of these minute freshwater crustaceans each day, swelling up to ten pounds or more in just a few seasons.

Fishing the Taylor tail water is technical and esoteric, with barely enough room between other anglers to swear under your breath without being heard. The most successful tactics and strategies—tiny subsurface mysis patterns, 8X tippets, pinch weights, and floating indicators—fail for even the most seasoned fly fishers of other fisheries in Colorado.

Aside from the tail water stretch, the Taylor is an excellent stream full of wild trout, and normal fly fishing tactics work on the freestone sections. The stream is framed by beautiful lodgepole pine, but the star of this show is the 0.4 miles of trophy water below the dam. To reach it, travel north from Almont on FR 742. You can't miss it. But if you do want to avoid that assembly line of anglers, the rest of the Taylor River is spectacularly decorated by nature, as it courses through a steep forested canyon, full of bouncy water and fighting fish. A float trip does it justice. Lottis Creek is a nice day diversion.

Royal Wulff

The more substantial tributary to La Jara Reservoir, Torsido Creek hosts approximately four short miles of quality wild brook trout fishing in extreme southern Colorado. Shallow, quiet, and with little riparian flora for cover along the lower two miles, Torsido's trout are easily spooked and dash for cover upon the slightest footfall or unnatural presence. A few Rio Grande cutthroats reside here, too.

Granitic rock formations appear like frozen globules of ancient clay to the north; to the south, open, uninterrupted vistas span the way to the cobalt blue reservoir. Fishing on

Torsido is peaceful, Zen-like, and always lonesome, with no need to ever step into the water and get your feet wet.

Finding this crystalline gem is another challenge altogether. Trimming the east side of La Jara Reservoir on the dirt road, veer back to the west on the branch of the road that crosses over the mesa toward the aspens, dropping down again on the other side of the rock formation. Hiking downstream a ways is best, because fishing from the inlet to the dense, canyon brush with hoppers, terrestrials, and attractors is productive from late spring through mid- to late summer.

Rubber-legged hare's ear beadhead

Adventurers will love this backcountry getaway. Located north of Pagosa Springs, this San Juan tributary provides several miles of pocket water angling for brook, rainbow, brown, and cutthroat trout. We like Turkey Creek because you can't drive along a road and park to fish. You must hike.

The fishing is good, not great, and the fish are wild and lively, but not large. So the payoff is the mobility—the movement into the wilderness, away from it all. Turkey Creek Trail has a good amount of traffic, mostly hikers and backpackers, with few anglers. You walk and huff and puff through a ponderosa pine and aspen forest. You'll stop off at a likely pool, catch a couple, and hike some more. The fish are pickier than you would think, so if the attractors aren't working, think caddis.

Drive north out of Pagosa Springs on U.S. 160. At about seven miles, you'll see Jackson Mountain Road (FR 37). Turn left and follow it to the trailhead.

Black woolly bugger

This is one of the more complex rivers in Colorado to explain. Located near Ridgway (which is north of Ouray, east of Telluride), the Uncompahgre, as a viable fishery, is a youngster. The river was decimated by mining over the years, but when Ridgway Reservoir was built in 1990, re-creating this river as a tail water in 1992 and filtering out the poison, the river became an overnight year-round sensation.

They tried stocking the tail water, especially with big brood fish, but the experiment didn't work for long. The state has since figured out what stocked trout work in this tail water and the fishing is boffo.

Ridgway State Park is the state's showoff park: modern, utilitarian, and clean. The best part of Uncompahgre, the tailrace, flows through Pa-Co-Chu-Puk Park, located below the lake. It's an odd place to fish. You have sidewalks and gazebos and bathrooms right along the river, like a Disney park. The green-tinted river has been constructed with weirs, manufactured pools, and carefully placed boulders. Everything is tidy and neat even though you are in a high-desert setting complete with deer, bears, and mountain lions, as well as piñon, oak, and ponderosa pine.

The two miles of river that run through Pa-Co-Chu-Puk are catch and release with easy access. Your heart will stop when you see some of the behemoths holding in the chutes below the weirs or in the deep pools. The predominant trout are rainbows and browns (with some cutthroats) but the stocking strategy of the river over the years keeps changing. You should stay out of this small-to-medium stream as much as possible, focusing on the pocket water, runs, riffles, pools, and edges. We do quite well working the banks.

Because Ridgway isn't near any major population centers, the relatively short stretch of water still provides more than enough trout. We're talking lots of catchable fish per mile. Because of the low elevation and the nature of tail waters, winter fly fishing is ideal. Try midges and blue-winged olives. Don't miss the pale morning dun hatch. Phenomenal. Caddis during summer. You sight fish much of the time on the Uncompahgre, but just because you see them doesn't mean they are easy. You need a daily state parks pass to enter and fish, and are allowed artificial flies only. Uncompahgre is about seven miles north of Ridgway on U.S. 550.

Uncompahgre River

Irresistible

The upper Rio Grande is a delightful full day-trip or camping getaway. You have a freestone stream in a wilderness setting with numerous tributaries. This is beautiful and rugged country. You'll be surrounded by dense spruce and aspen forests and tall canyon ridges. Deep runs, big pools, riffles, all kinds of water flowing through narrow canyons and broad valleys.

We've scuffed up our car doors, broken off door mirrors, and spooked resting elk as we maneuvered through willows and had days where we should have been embarrassed with how many trout we caught (but we weren't). The upper stretches of the Rio Grande, above and below the reservoirs, are classic small- to medium-stream western angling. Set up camp, fish the Rio Grande, and make sure to venture to such stalwart feeder creeks as Pole, Ute, Big Squaw, and Little Squaw.

The upper river can be reached by traveling south on CO 149 from Lake City and then west on FR 520 (the Rio Grande Reservoir Road). Road Canyon Campground is located just west of the reservoir. FR 520 runs alongside the upper river for much of its course, and this forest service road is an often bumpy, rough dirt road, strewn with big rocks and deep potholes throughout. A four-wheel-drive vehicle is a must. From FR 520, anglers can reach the river and its headwaters by hiking the trails, of which there are many.

Melonhead beadhead

We've never fished a clearer creek. The water is often so invisible, it's like an optical illusion. The fish are wild and plentiful but not especially large. The fun in this stream is the beauty of it all, the wildness, the multicolored rock riverbed, and the alternating meadow and canyon sections.

Located northeast of Durango, Vallecito Creek flows quickly from its headwaters, rushing toward its impoundment at Vallecito Reservoir. You'll find plenty of traffic on the trail along the creek but they're mostly hikers and backpackers, not anglers. Vallecito is perfect for dry fly fishing since the rainbows, brookies, and cutthroats are not hatch-dependent and instead are voraciously opportunistic. The closer to the trailhead you fish, the more traffic. Keep moving upstream. The first couple of miles from the trailhead will be steep climbing and away from the stream. You get wide flats, riffles, deep drop pools, and twenty miles of river to yourself.

Strap on a day pack or fanny pack containing water and a lunch, start your trek, and enjoy a full day's fishing on a true high-country, pristine creek located almost totally in the Weminuche Wilderness. Another great option is to backpack along the twenty-two miles of trails and streams. From the valley upstream, you can fish up any number of feeder creeks or hike on up to some awesome alpine lakes. Around the big, popular campground near the trailhead, you'll enjoy ponderosa pine, Gambel oak, and aspen forests.

Vallecito Creek

Lime trude

Twenty-two miles north of Pagosa Springs lies one of the most beautiful spots in all of the Rockies. Williams Creek Reservoir could possibly be the most magnificent setting we've encountered on any of our trips. Surrounded by three major peaks, the craggy summits seem to scrape their way out of the earth before your very eyes. The impoundment fills up from the cold headwaters of Williams Creek. Below the lake flows the tail water version, which is small, intimate, and easy to fish. Not only is the area a family camping paradise, but this Piedra River feeder stream is a tail water that's fishable for rainbows, brookies, and browns nine months out of the year. The lower stretches are mostly open with cottonwoods and scattered stands of ponderosa pine and aspen.

We've fished the tail water two dozen times, maybe more. We always have to leapfrog slow, clumsy anglers (many fishing downstream). We always catch brookies but we don't always catch both browns and rainbows. Either-or, it seems. When we get into the browns, one of us always catches a pretty decent one. We stay away from below the spillway except in the late evening when some nice hatches come off and the tailrace comes alive with surface feeders.

Williams Creek offers good angling from the spillway to its confluence with the Piedra. The campgrounds are lightly shaded by aspens or heavily shaded by dense stands of Douglas fir. Above the lake, the creek is much smaller, very cold, and full of small brooks and surprisingly fat cutthroats. That's all we can say about that. The trail doesn't really follow the river so it's just easier to wade upriver or walk alongside it. From Pagosa Springs, take Piedra Road north a long ways, close to twenty miles. At one point, Piedra Road turns into a gravel-dirt road and is called FR 631.

Elk hair caddis

West of the Collegiate Peaks, beginning simply as several trickles of water converging near the wee town of Tincup, Willow Creek abruptly forms into one of Taylor Park's unsung fisheries. A gold miner named Jim Taylor (for whom many area landmarks are named) harvested gold nuggets from Willow Creek in a "tin cup," spurring a short-lived rush and bringing notoriety to the region.

Today, Taylor Reservoir's tail water brings the valley its notoriety. But when anglers tire of world-class fishing for huge trout, the numerous bend pools, beaver ponds, and cut banks of Willow Creek come as a quiet relief. We adored it so much we chose a picture of Willow Creek for the cover of another of our books.

After a brief high-mountain rain shower dampened the scrub brush, I observed from my camp chair as Williams worked this bend pool like a determined technician. Trout were rising one after the other, desperate to take his fly, but kept missing, as though drunk from the sudden shower. Finally, after almost fifteen minutes of "ohs" and "ahs" one finally stuck himself on Williams's Royal Wulff. When they're rising on Willow Creek, keep after them.

From Almont, travel north on FR 742 along the famed Taylor River until the road hooks right just past the Taylor Park Trading Post, crossing over Willow Creek and skirting it for several miles.

Willow Creek